First published in Great Britain 2013 by
COTTONTHREAD BOOKS, an imprint of
Penny and Penny
135 Bay View Road, Northam
Devon EX39 1BJ
www.pennyandpenny.co.uk

ISBN: 978-0-9576659-0-3

Created, designed and produced in the UK
Printed by Remous Ltd

SMALL AND PRETTY

SUSAN PENNY

www.cottonthreadbooks.co.uk

CONTENTS

Most of the projects in *Quick Knits Small and Pretty* use less than a ball of wool, so they are a great way of using up what you have in your scrap bag. You could also try recycling knitted garments that you or your family have outgrown. To do this, first wash the garment and then, when dry, unravel the wool from the cast-off edge. Discard any worn wool, then rewind into skeins. Tie each skein at the top and the bottom. Wet, and then hang from a hook or peg to dry with a weight attached to the bottom. Once dry, the kinks will be removed and the wool will be ready to start a new life as a hand-knitted keepsake.

If you would like more information on recycling wool, have problems with a pattern in this book, or just want to check out what we are working on next, then please go to www.pennyandpenny.co.uk for up-to-date information and pages of ideas and inspiration.

HELLO

Do you find yourself unable to buy stylish, easy-to-knit designs? Are you looking for patterns that you can knit up in just a few hours? Whether you are a beginner or more experienced knitter, discover lots of new ideas to keep your needles busy in *Quick Knits Small and Pretty*. Most of the patterns in this book are made using basic knitting instructions, but where they are more involved, the technique is thoroughly explained. This allows you to master it quickly and then move on with your knitting. Easy-to-use and just the right size to take anywhere, *Quick Knits Small and Pretty* is an essential resource for anyone wanting new and imaginative knitting projects.

Inspired by the success of *Knitted Cakes*, I wanted to write a book of small projects that would have a broader appeal. Most of the patterns can be knitted with scraps of left-over wool. Experiment with anything you have to hand but remember to change the needle size to give an even tension. This way the stuffing will not show through. I have written each of the 21 projects in a no-nonsense 'how-to' way, with useful hints and tips. Three are cakes, and the rest are an eclectic mix of useful and pretty, making *Quick Knits Small and Pretty* a great book for the serious and the weekend knitter. So if you're feeling motivated, just turn the page and start knitting – and in just a few hours you will have completed your first project!

Susan Penny

KNITTING ABBREVIATIONS

Beg: begin; begins; beginning
dec: decrease; decreasing
DK: double knitting
dp; dpn: double-pointed needle
g st: garter stitch
inc: increase; increasing
inc1: increase (by working into the front and back of the stitch)
inc2: knit into front, back and front of stitch
k: knit
knit: knit
kfb: knit into the front and back of stitch
k2tog: knit two together
kwise: knitwise
m1: make one stitch
p: purl
psso: pass the slipped stitch over

p2tog: purl two stitches together
pwise: purlwise
rem: remain; remaining
rep: repeat
RS: right side
sl: slip
sl1: slip one stitch on to the right hand needle without knitting it
sl st: slip stitch
st; sts: stitch; stitches
St st: stocking stitch (one knit row, one purl row)
tbl: through back loop
tog: together
WS: wrong side
yf (or yfwd): yarn to the front (or forward)
yon: yarn over needle

KNITTING NOTES

Knitting Terminology

cont in pat: Continue to work the pattern as previously described.

cont in this way: Continue to work as previously described.

double ended needles: Needles without end stops that will allow you to slide your knitting to either end.

casting off: When casting off, pull the yarn through the last loop on the needle to finish the piece and stop it unravelling.

inc ... sts evenly across row: Increase the stitches at even intervals across the row.

knitwise : Insert the needle into the stitch as if you were going to knit it.

next row (RS), or (WS): The row following the one you have just worked will be a right side (or wrong side) row.

on all foll rows: An instruction that applies to all the rows following the row just worked.

purlwise: Insert the needle into the stitch as if you were going to purl it.

rep from * to *: Repeat the instructions that begin at the first asterisk and end at the next.

rep from ... row: Repeat the pattern rows previously worked, beginning with the row specified.

rep ... times more: Repeat an instruction the number of times given (not counting the first time you work it).

right side (or RS): Refers to the surface of the work that will face outwards.

row: One horizontal line of stitches.

thumb method of casting on: Use one needle and wrap the wool around your thumb.

with RS facing: The right side of the work is facing you and wrong side facing away.

with WS facing: A term used when the wrong side of the work must be facing you and the right side facing away from you.

work rep of chart ... times: When working a pattern from a chart, work the stitches in the repeat as many times as indicated.

work to end: Work the pattern to the end of the row.

work to last ... sts: Work across the row until the specified number of stitches remain on the needle.

wrong side (or WS): Refers to the surface of the work that will be on the inside of the knitting.

MAKING A BOBBLE

Cut a length of wool to hold the bobble together (the fastener), and lay it along a pencil. Wind another longer length of wool around and around the pencil for about 3cm (1¼in). Pull the fastener ends together and tie loosely to hold the loops of wool firmly in place. Slip off the pencil. Cut through the loops and then knot the fastener tightly. Trim the bobble neatly and sew it in place.

MAKING THE I-CORD

Cast on 3 sts using double ended needles. Knit across the row. Slip your stitches to the other end of the needle and knit into the first stitch, pulling up tightly to form a cord. Knit the other two stitches, then slide the knitting along the needle and repeat. You will need to pull the wool tightly on your first stitch or you will not make a neat cord. Continue until the correct length is reached. Cast off.

KNITTING NOTES

MATTRESS STITCH

With RS facing, and with knitted pieces side by side, pull the edge stitch slightly away from the stitch next to it. You will see a horizontal bar. Insert your needle under the bar. Pull the wool loosely through, then insert the needle under the parallel horizontal bar on the other piece. Work back and forth for a short distance and then gently pull the yarn in the direction of the seam, closing the gap.

FRENCH KNOT

Bring the needle and yarn out of the knitting at the point where you want the knot to be. Holding the wool taut, and with the needle pointing away from the fabric, wrap the wool around the needle several times. Insert the needle back into the knitting close to where the wool emerged. Pull up the wool to tighten the knot, and then take the needle back through to the WS of the knitting.

STAR STITCH

Thread a large-eyed needle with wool, and starting with a knot on the WS of the knitting, bring the needle out at 1. Insert the needle back into the knitting at 2. Continue in this way following the numbers until you have completed the star. Take the needle back through the knitting to the WS at 8 and finish on the back with a few stitches. You can make a longer star by extending the length of 1 to 2.

LAZY DAISY

Starting with a knot on the WS, bring the needle out at the base of a petal. Insert the needle back into the knitting a short distance away and then come out again at the top of the petal. Make a loop with the wool, taking it behind the needle. Pull the needle out of the knitting and make a small stitch over the top of the petal to hold it in place. Lazy daisy stitches can be worked from a central point, in rows or individually.

7

DAISY EGG COSY

This charming egg cosy will keep your morning boiled egg nice and warm until you are ready to eat breakfast

Materials:
Double knitting wool – sea green, white flecked, yellow

Needles:
1 pair 4mm (UK 8; US 6) knitting needles

Instructions:

Egg cosy
Cast on 33 sts using sea green double knitting wool and 4mm needles.
Row 1–12: knit.
Row 13–24: work in st st starting with a purl row.
Break yarn, leaving a long end. Thread through the stitches on the needle, pull up tightly and secure.

Daisy
Make six petals.
Work one petal at a time and then join together using the instructions below.

*Using white flecked wool place a slip knot onto your needle and then cast on 4 sts.
Cast off 4 sts.
Break yarn and pull it through the remaining stitch.
Finish the ends by carefully weaving them into the petal.*
Make six petals working each one from * to *.

Try to keep all the petals facing in the same direction until they are stitched together. Run a length of wool through the straight edge at the top of each petal and then draw up the thread tightly to form a flower. Secure the ends with a knot and leave uncut.

Daisy centre
Cast on 1 st using yellow wool, knit into the front, back, front, back and front of the stitch [5 sts].

Row 1: turn and knit row.
Row 2: purl.
Row 3: knit.
Row 4: purl.
Row 5: k3tog, k2tog.
Break yarn and thread it through remaining 2 sts.
Using the wool end left at the centre of the assembled daisy, stitch the daisy centre in place.

Butterfly wings
Knit two wings in white flecked wool using the instructions given above for the petal, working from * to *. Turn the wings so that they are facing in opposite directions.

Butterfly body
To make the body of the butterfly, working with one needle, make a slip knot in yellow wool. With the needle in your right hand, wrap the wool around the needle and knit the stitch to make one chain. While you are making the chain length you will have only one stitch on your needle and the construction will be similar to a crochet chain. Make sure that each chain remains tight. Continue until the chain length is just longer than the wings when placed between them. Cut the thread and slip it through the stitch. Unravel the wool ends to form two antennae. Stitch the wings either side of the butterfly body.

Making up
Using the long wool end left at the top of the egg cosy, sew up the back seam on the wrong side of the knitting. Turn the cosy through to the right side. Sew the daisy to the top and the butterfly onto the side of the egg cosy.

BEACH HUT PAPERWEIGHT

Conjure up memories of sunny days spent on the beach with this nautically-inspired beach hut on your desk

Materials:
Merino knitting wool – blue, white, pink
Button
Cardboard box – 6 cm wide x 4 cm deep x 12.5cm high(2⅛x1⅝x5in)
Dried rice in a plastic bag

Needles:
1 pair 3.25mm (UK 10; US 3) knitting needles
1 pair 3.25mm (UK 10; US 3) double-ended knitting needles

Instructions:

Front & back – knit both the same.
Cast on 16 sts using blue merino knitting wool and 3.25mm needles, work in st st.
Row 1–4: st st in blue wool for 4 rows.
Row 5–8: change to white wool and work 4 rows in st st.
Row 9–12: change to blue wool and work 4 rows in st st.
Row 13–16: change to white wool work 4 rows in st st.
Row 17–20: change to blue wool and work 4 rows in st st.
Row 21–24: change to white wool and work 4 rows in st st.
Row 25–28: change to blue wool and work 4 rows in st st.
Row 29: change to white wool. k2tog, k to last 2 sts, k2tog [14 sts].
Row 30: purl.
Row 31: k2tog, k to last 2 sts, k2tog [12 sts].
Row 32: purl.
Row 33: change to blue wool. k2tog, k to last 2 sts, k2tog [10 sts].
Row 34: purl.
Row 35: k2tog, k to last 2 sts, k2tog [8 sts].
Row 36: purl.
Row 37: change to white wool. k2tog, k to last 2 sts, k2tog [6 sts].
Row 38: purl.
Row 39: k2tog, k to last 2 sts, k2tog [4 sts].

Row 40: purl.
Break wool, leaving a long end. Thread through the stitches on the needle and draw up tightly.

Sides and bottom – knitted as one.
Cast on 9 sts using white merino knitting wool and 3.25mm needles, work in st st.
Row 1–36: st st starting with white wool, change colour every 4 rows to match the stripes on the beach hut front and back.
Row 37–62: change to blue wool and st st 26 rows in blue – this will create the bottom with the lower blue stripe on either side attached.
Row 63–98: change to white wool. St st 36 rows changing colour every 4 rows to match the stripes on the beach hut front and back.
Cast off.

Roof
Cast on 14 sts using blue merino knitting wool and 3.25mm needles.
Row 1–40: work in st st for 40 rows without changing colour.
Cast off.

Door
Cast on 7 sts using pink merino knitting wool and 3.25mm needles.
Row 1–30: work in st st for 30 rows without changing colour.
Cast off.

Bargeboard – knit two.
Cast on 3 sts using pink merino knitting wool and 3.25mm needles.
Row 1–38: work in st st for 38 rows without changing colour.
Cast off.

i–cord base
Cast on 3 sts using double-ended needles. Knit across the row. Slip your stitches to the other end of the needle and knit into the first stitch, pulling tight to form a cord. Knit the

other two stitches, slide the knitting along and repeat. You will need to pull the wool tight on your first stitch or you will not make a neat cord. Continue in this way until your i–cord is long enough to go completely around the bottom of the beach hut.

Making up
If you cannot find a box that's the correct size to make the beach hut, use the outline on page 48 to build one. Before you seal the bottom of the box, insert a plastic bag filled with rice to give the beach hut weight. Pin the knitted sections onto the cardboard shape to check the fit. Working on the wrong side of the knitting, stitch the front and back sections to the sides, working down the roof and then down the sides. Sew the front to the base, leaving the back at the bottom edge open for turning. Turn through the gap to the right side of the knitting. Insert the cardboard beach hut through the gap at the bottom, and then sew up the seam. Lay the roof in place and sew it to the beach hut with small stitches. Sew the pink knitted bargeboard to the front and back of the roof. Pin the door to the beach hut front, and then stitch firmly in place. Sew a button onto the door for a handle. Pin and then sew the i–cord around the base of the beach hut.

CELEBRATION CAKE

Whatever the occasion, this delightful knitted cake is sure to please. It's good to look at and guaranteed calorie-free

Materials:
Double knitting wool – raspberry, chocolate, cream, mauve, lilac
Fluffy polyester yarn –cream
Seed beads – mixed colours
Drinking straw
Toy stuffing
Cardboard food container with plastic lid used for storing gravy granules or other dried food – 9cm (3½in) diameter

Needles:
1 pair 3.25mm (UK 10; US 3) knitting needles

Instructions:

Side of cake
Cast on 56 sts using raspberry double knitting wool and 4mm needles.
Row 1–4: work in st st.
Row 5–6: change to chocolate and continue in st st.
Row 7–8: change back to raspberry and continue in st st.
Row 9–12: work in st st, using the fluffy yarn. If the yarn is very fine then use it with the cream double knitting wool, working both strands together.
Row 13–14: change to raspberry and work in st st.
Row 15–16: change to chocolate and work in st st.
Row 17–20: change to raspberry and work in st st.
Cast off.

Bottom and top of cake
Make two circles.
Cast on 8 sts. Work in st st.
Row 1: inc2, knit to last 2 sts, inc2 [12 sts].
Row 2: inc2, purl to last 2 sts, inc2 [16 sts].
Row 3: inc1, knit to last st, inc1 [18 sts].
Row 4: purl.
Row 5: inc1, knit to last st, inc1 [20 sts].

Row 6: purl.
Row 7: knit.
Row 8: purl.
Row 9: inc1, knit to last st, inc1 [22 sts].
Row 10–20: st st the next 11 rows, starting with a purl.
Row 21: dec1, knit to last st, dec1 [20 sts].
Row 22–24: st st for 3 rows starting with a purl.
Row 25: dec1, knit to last st, dec1 [18 sts].
Row 26: purl.
Row 27: dec1, knit to last st, dec1 [16 sts].
Row 28: dec2, purl to last 2 sts, dec2 [12 sts].
Row 29: dec2, knit to last 2 sts, dec2 [8 sts].
Cast off.

Piped cream
Make two lengths of piped cream, one with 14 cream swirls and the other with 17 swirls.

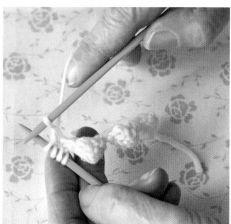

To make a single cream swirl, cast on 1 st using cream wool.
*Row 1: k1, p1, k1, p1, k1 into the cast on stitch [5 sts].
Row 2: slip 1, k3, leave the last stitch unworked.
Work on the 3 centre stitches until row 6.
Row 3: p3, leave last st.
Row 4: k3, leave last st.

Continued on page 14

CELEBRATION CAKE

Row 5: p3, leave last st.
Row 6: k4.
Row 7: p1, p2tog, p2tog.
Row 8: k2tog, k1.
Row 9: p2tog [1 st].*
This makes a single cream swirl. Repeat from * to * until you have the required lengths. Break yarn and pull through the remaining stitch.

Cake balls
Cast on 6 sts in cream, raspberry, mauve or lilac wool.
Row 1: knit into the front and back of every stitch [12 sts].
Row 2: purl.
Row 3: knit.
Row 4, 6, 8: purl.
Row 5, 7: knit
Row 9: knit 2tog to end [6 sts].
Break yarn and pull through the remaining stitches. Pull up tightly and fasten.

Candle
Cast on 17 sts in cream wool.
Row 1–7: work in garter stitch. Cast off.

Flame
Cast on 2 sts in raspberry wool and work in garter stitch.
Row 1: knit.
Row 2: inc into every stitch [4 sts].
Row 3–4: knit.
Row 5: inc 1 st at the beginning and end of the row [6 sts].
Row 6–7: knit.
Row 8: k2tog, k2, k2tog [4 sts].
Row 9–10: knit.
Row 11: k2tog, k2tog [2 sts].
Row 12: k2tog.

Making up
You will need a tubular cardboard food container with a plastic lid – the sort used to store gravy granules or similar dry food stuff. Remove the plastic lid and cut the height of the container down to 6.5cm (2½in). Glue the plastic lid back onto container, filling it with rice or beads if you want to make the cake heavier. Turn the container over so that the plastic lid becomes the base of the cake.

Make a small hole in the cake top with a sharp point to insert the candle at a later stage. Wrap the knitted cake side around the container and stitch it together at the side seam. Pin and then stitch the top and bottom of the cake in place. Pin and then stitch the piped cream around the top and the bottom edges of the cake – the longer length of piped cream is for the bottom of the cake. Wrap the knitted candle around the straw and stitch it in place down the side seam and across the top. Carefully find the hole in the cake top through the knitting and then, using a knitting needle, make the hole slightly bigger, easing the straw into the cake. Stitch the knitted candle to the cake top to hold it firmly in place. Stitch the flame to the top of the candle and then add a red bead for the centre of the flame. Stitch up the side seam of a cake ball, stuffing it well before finally closing the seam. Sew seed beads to the surface of the ball. Repeat for the other balls and then pile them around the candle on the cake top.

FLOWER BROOCH

Easy to knit in 4 ply mohair, these attractive flower brooches sparkle when decorated with vintage beads

Materials:
4 ply mohair knitting wool – mauve, lavender
Felt – mauve
Beads
Brooch back or hair clip

Needles:
1 pair 4mm (UK 8; US 6) knitting needles

Instructions:

Cast on 8 sts using 4 ply knitting wool and 4mm needles.
Knit in garter stitch until the work measures 33cm (13in). Cast off.

Making up
Fold the strip of knitting in half lengthways, and using a needle threaded with wool, sew the two layers together down the sides and along the long edge. At one end on the bottom edge run a row of gathering stitches for about 5cm (2in). Pull up the thread and secure with a few stitches. Starting at the gathered end, wind the knitting around like a snail shell and then, working from the back, stitch the coil securely together. To make the petal shapes, stitch over the coil two or three times to pull the knitting in and then secure on the back. Repeat at several points around the coil. To strengthen the back of the flower, cut a 6cm (2⅜in) circle from felt. Glue this to the back of your knitted flower. Cut a small circle of felt to fit into the centre of your flower and decorate with beads. Glue or stitch the decorated felt circle in place. Stitch a brooch back or hair clip to the back of the flower.

BALLERINA TEDDY

This teddy is knitted in one piece and then folded over at the top. Once assembled the skirt is added using net

Materials:
Merino knitting wool – cream, pink and grey
Toy stuffing
Net for the tutu
Ribbon for teddy's neck
Small amount of wool to embroider the
teddy's face – brown, black

Needles:
1 pair 4mm (UK 8; US 6) knitting needles

Instructions:
Please note – this teddy is knitted in one piece
with the fold at the top of his head.

Legs
Starting at the bottom of one leg, cast on 10
sts in grey wool. Work in st st.
Row 1–6: knit in st st.
Row 7–20: change to cream wool and
continue in st st. Put these 10 sts onto a clip.
Cast on 10 sts in grey wool and make a second
leg.

Body, arms and head
Put both legs onto the same pair of needles
with the RS facing you.
Row 1–10: change to pink wool and knit
across both legs. Continue in st st for 10 rows.
Row 11: cast on 6 sts in pink (arm) and 4 sts in
cream (paw) at beg of the row, then k to the
end of the row [30 sts].
Row 12: cast on 6 sts in pink (arm) and 4 sts in
cream (paw) at beg of the row, then p to the
end of the row [40 sts].
Row 13: k4 cream, k32 pink, k4 cream.
Row 14: p4 cream, p32 pink, p4 cream.
Row 15: *k4 cream, k12 pink, k8 cream, k12
pink, k4 cream.
Row 16: p4 cream, p12 pink, p8 cream, p12
pink, p4 cream.*
Rows 17–20: repeat rows 15 and 16 from * to *
twice more.
Row 21: (cast off 4 sts in cream, 8 sts in pink)

(k4 pink, k8 cream, k4 pink – neck) (Cast off 8
sts pink, 4 sts cream).
Row 22: join in cream wool and p across row
[16 sts].
Row 23–32: continue in st st for 10 rows.
Row 33: cast on 2 sts at the beginning of the
row, k to the end.
Row 34: cast on 2 sts at the beginning of the
row, p to the end [20 sts].
Row 35–38: st st.
You have now reached the top of the teddy.
Continuing on the same stitches, following the
pattern down the back.
Row 39–42: st st.
Row 43: dec 2 sts at the beginning of the row,
k to the end.
Row 44: dec 2 sts at the beginning of the row,
p to the end [16 sts].
Row 45–54: continue in st st for 10 rows.
Row 55: cast on 8 sts in pink (arm) and 4 sts in
cream (paw) at beg of row. k 4 cream, k24 pink.
Row 56: cast on 8 sts in pink (arm) and 4 sts
in cream (paw) at beg of row. p4 cream, p32
pink, p4 cream [40 sts].
Row 57: *k4 cream, k32 pink, k4 cream.
Row 58: p4 cream, p32 pink, p4 cream.*
Row 59–64: repeat from * to * three more times.
Row 65: cast off 4 sts in cream, 6 sts in pink,
knit to last 10 sts. Cast off 6 sts in pink, 4 sts in
cream [20 sts].
Row 66–74: change to pink wool and work in
st st for 9 rows.

Split for the legs
Work on the first 10 sts only, putting the last
10 sts on a clip.
Row 1–13: st st 13 rows in cream wool.
Row 14–20: change to grey wool and knit 7
rows in st st.
Cast off on a purl row and then repeat for the
other leg using the stitches held on the clip.

Making up
On the wrong side of the knitting, fold the
teddy in half at the top of his head. Sew

around the teddy shape, leaving a gap for turning from the underarm down the side of her leg. Stitch slightly in at the corners of the paws to give a nice rounded shape. Stuff teddy and sew up the gap. Make two French knots for the teddy's eyes using brown wool, and a button nose and mouth in long stitch using black wool – see page 48 for a trace of teddy's face detail. Using cream wool, stitch across the corner of both ears to create a triangular shape. With the same coloured wool make a row of small gathering stitches around teddy's neck, pull up and then fasten the thread firmly. Cover the gathering stitches with a ribbon bow. For the tutu, cut lengths of pink net 12cm long x 3cm wide (4¾ x1¼in). Thread one end of the net through a large-eyed needle and make a stitch at teddy's waist. Remove the needle, and with the net ends the same length, tie a knot in the net to hold it firmly in place. Continue adding net until you have gone right around teddy's waist.

ROSE HEADBAND

For a lovely timeless wedding-day look, knit these pretty flowers in shades to match your bridesmaids' dresses

Materials:
4 ply wool – shades of mauve
4 ply wool – green for the leaves
Headband
Ponytail band

Needles:
1 pair 3.25mm (UK 10; US3) knitting needles

Instructions:

Roses
Cast on 10 sts using pink wool and 3.25mm needles. Work in st st.
Row 1: knit.
Row 2: purl.
Row 3: knit increasing every stitch [20 sts].
Row 4: purl.
Row 5: knit, increasing in every stitch [40 sts].
Row 6: purl.
Row 7: knit, increasing every stitch [80 sts].
Row 8: purl.

Row 9: knit, increasing every fourth stitch across the row [100 sts].
Cast off.

Leaves
Cast on 3 sts and work in g st.
Row 1: knit.
Row 2: knit into the front and back of every stitch [6 sts].
Row 3–4: knit.
Row 5: inc 1 at the beg and end of row [8 sts].
Row 6–7: knit.
Row 8: k2tog at beginning and end of the row [6 sts].
Row 9–10: knit.
Row11: k2tog at beginning and end of the row [4 sts].
Row 12: k2tog, k2tog.
Break yarn and pull it through stitches.

To make up the roses
Allow each knitted rose to curl up into a pleasing shape. Secure at the centre with a

few neat stitches. Sew two leaves to the back of each rose. For the headband, attach two roses, stitching securely over the headband several times to hold them in place. Assemble the ponytail band in the same way, stitching through the elastic band.

These pretty roses would make a lovely bridesmaid's coronet. Make a circular framework from florist's wire wrapped in white florist's tape. Attach ivory knitted roses for a vintage look.

STRIPED MITTENS

These fun mittens are easy to make and they will keep you warm and snuggly on even the coldest winter's day

Materials:
Double knitting wool – cream, green
Vintage buttons – six
Green fabric bow for each mitten

Needles:
1 pair 4mm (UK 8; US 6) knitting needles

Instructions:

Cast on 44 sts at the cuff edge using cream double knitting wool and 4mm needles.
Row 1–2: k1, p1, to the end of the row.
Change to green wool. Repeat these two rows a further six times, changing wool colour after you have worked each set of two rows to create stripes – 14 rows worked for the cuff.
To knit the mittens, change back to green wool and work 16 rows in st st starting with a knit row and ending with a purl. Next, work either the left or the right thumb hole, the instructions are given below.

Right hand thumb hole
Next row: k30 sts cast off 7 sts, knit to the end of the row.
Next row: p7, cast on 7 sts, purl to the end of the row.

Left hand thumb hole
Next row: k7, cast off 7sts, knit to the end of the row.
Next row: p30, cast on 7 sts, purl to the end of the row.

Both mittens
Work 6 rows of st st starting with a knit row and ending with a purl.

Mitten top
Change to cream wool.
Next row: *k1, p1 to the end of the row.
Next row: k1, p1 to the end of the row.*
Repeat these two rows from * to * twice more,

changing wool colour after every two rows to create stripes – 6 rows.
Next row: k1, p1 to the end of the row.
Cast off in the rib pattern.

Making up
Neaten any wool ends. Fold the mitten and then join the long seam using mattress stitch – the seam will sit on the palm of your hand and will not show. Put the mitten on your hand and then place the button and the bow at the wrist edge before sewing securely in place with green wool.

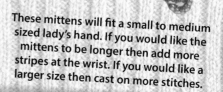

These mittens will fit a small to medium sized lady's hand. If you would like the mittens to be longer then add more stripes at the wrist. If you would like a larger size then cast on more stitches.

JAM TART SLICE

Several slices of this colourful knitted jam tart would look great displayed together on a glass cake stand

Materials:
Double knitting wool – red, beige
Buttons – red, cream
Cardboard for insert
Toy stuffing

Needles:
1 pair 3.25mm (UK 10; US3) knitting needles

Instructions:

Base and back of pastry case
Cast on 18 sts in beige wool using 3.25mm needles.
Row 1–8: work in st st, starting with a k row.
Row 9: purl across a knit row.
Rows 10–16: work in st st, starting with a purl row.
Row 17: k1, k2tog, k to last 3 sts, k2tog, k1 [16 sts].
Rows 18–20: work in st st, starting with a purl row.
Row 21: K1, k2 tog, k to last 3 sts, k2tog, k1 [14 sts].
Rows 22–24: work in st st, starting with a purl row.
Row 25: k1, k2tog, k to last 3 sts, k2tog, k1 [12 sts].
Rows 26–28: work in st st, starting with a purl row.
Row 29: k1, k2tog, k to last 3 sts, k2tog, k1 [10 sts].
Row 30–32: work in st st, starting with a purl row.
Row 33: k1, k2tog, k to last 3 sts, k2tog, k1 [8 sts].
Row 34: purl.
Row 35: k1, k2tog, k to last 3 sts, k2tog, k1 [6 sts].
Row 36: purl.
Row 37: k1, k2tog, k2tog, k1 [4 sts].
Row 38: purl.
Row 39: k2tog, k2tog [2 sts].
Row 40: purl.

Row 41: k2tog.
Break the wool, leaving a long end. Thread through last stitch on needle.

Sides of tart
Pick up and knit 31 sts in beige wool along one edge of the triangular pastry case base.
Row 2: purl.
Row 3–9: change to red wool and work in st st for 7 rows.
Cast off on a purl row. Repeat on the other side of the pastry case.

Pastry crust
Make three pastry swirls using beige wool using the instructions given below.
Cast on 1 st in beige wool.
Row 1: * k1 p1, k1, p1, k1 into the cast–on stitch [5 sts].
Row 2: slip 1, k3, leave the last stitch unworked. Work on the 3 centre stitches until row 6.
Row 3: p3, leave last stitch.
Row 4: k3, leave last stitch.
Row 5: p3 leave last stitch.
Row 6: k4.
Row 7: p1, p2tog twice.
Row 8: k2tog, k1.
Row 9: p2tog. * [1 st]
Break yarn and pull it through the remaining stitch. This makes a pastry swirl. Repeat rows 1–9 from * to * to make the three swirls.

Top of tart
Cast on 18 sts in red.
Rows 1–5: work in st st, starting with a purl row.
Row 6: k1, k2tog, k to last 3 sts, k2tog, k1 [16 sts].
Rows 7–9: work in st st, starting with a purl row.
Row 10: k1, k2 tog, k to last 3sts, k2tog, k1 [14 sts].
Rows 11–13: work in st st, starting with a purl row.

22

Continued on page 24

JAM TART SLICE

Row 28: k3tog.
Break yarn, leaving a long end. Thread through last stitch on needle.

Making up
On the wrong side of the knitting, stitch the front edges of the tart together to form a point, and the sides of the tart to the back edge. Cut a strip of cardboard the same height as the tart and long enough to fit along the two sides and across the back. Fold the strip into a triangular shape to line the tart and stick together with tape. It is important to make the cardboard shape a little larger than the tart so that the knitting will be slightly stretched - this will give a neater finish.

Row 14: k1, k2tog, k to last 3sts, k2tog, k1 [12 sts].
Rows 15–17: work in st st, starting with a purl row.
Row 18: k1, k2tog, K to last 3 sts, k2 tog, k1 [10 sts].
Row 19–21: work in st st, starting with a purl row.
Row 22: k1, k2tog 4 times, k1 [6 sts].
Row 23: purl.
Row 24: knit.
Row 25: purl.
Row 26: k2tog 3 times [3 sts].
Row 27: purl

Use a variety of old buttons to finish the top of the jam tart.

Cut a triangle from cardboard to fit into the bottom of the tart. Use tape to stick this to the cardboard sides. Insert the cardboard liner into the bottom of the knitted tart. Fill with toy stuffing. Place the knitted top on the tart and stitch in place. Finish by sewing the pastry crust to the back edge and also sewing the buttons to the top of the tart.

MOLLY DOLLY

This cute little doll can easily be made into a brooch by attaching a pin to the back

Materials:
4 ply knitting wool – pink, blue, mauve
Double knitting wool – for arms and legs
Small beads
Dolls hair or wool for plaits
Small rubber bands
Wooden button or disc
Permanent marker pen – black, red

Needles:
1 pair 3.25mm (UK 10; US 3) knitting needles

Instructions:

Dress
Cast on 26 sts using 4 ply wool and 3.25mm needles.
Row 1–14: st st.
Break yarn, leaving a long end. Thread through the stitches on the needle. Pull the wool up tightly and secure with a few stitches on the back of the knitting.

Hat
Cast on 12 sts using 4 ply wool and 3.25mm needles.
Row 1–3: knit.
Row 4–8: st st starting with a purl.
Row 9: k2tog across the row [6 sts].
Break yarn, leaving a long end. Thread through the stitches on the needle. Pull the wool up tightly and secure as before.

Making up
On the wrong side of the dress, sew up the back seam carefully. The top should already be pulled together and secured. Turn the dress through to the right side. To make the waist, wrap a length of wool several times around the dress, pulling the thread tight and then weaving the end into the knitting. Sew up the back seam of the hat on the reverse side of the knitting in the same way as the dress. Sew a bead to the point of the hat. Using either doll hair or wool for the hair, make a 10cm (4in) plait and then secure both ends with small elastic bands - these can be bought from a hair accessory shop. Fold the plait in half and glue the fold to the back of the wooden disc or button. Use a permanent marker pen to draw eyes and a small mouth on to the front of the disc or button. Position the hat in place and glue, taking care not to cover the eyes. Using double knitting wool cut six lengths about 20cm (8in) long. Tie a knot at one end and plait the wool working two strands together for approximately 6cm (2⅜in). Tie a knot in the other end and trim the wool at both ends close to the knot. Fold the plait in half and stitch to the inside of the doll's dress as high as you can. Make a 3cm (1¼in) plait for the arms and stitch the centre of the plait to the back of the knitted dress just above waist level. Finally, glue the head to the neck edge of the dress, holding it in place with pins until the joint is completely dry.

RED ROSE

Give this pretty red rose to someone very special in your life
and you can be sure it will be a bloom that lasts forever

Materials:
Double knitting wool – red
Thin jewellery wire – red, or silver florist's wire
Green florist's tape
Pearl bead
Red glitter

Needles:
1 pair 3.25mm (UK 10; US3) knitting needles

Instructions:

Central petal
Knit one petal.
Cast on 10sts in red wool using 3.25mm
needles.
Row 1–3: knit
Row 4–7: knit, increasing one stitch at the
beginning of the each row [14 sts].
Row 8–15: knit.
Row 16–17: knit, decreasing one stitch at the
beginning of each row [12 sts].
Row 18: knit.
Row 19–20: knit, decreasing one stitch at the
beginning of each row [10 sts].
Row 21: k2tog, knit to last 2sts, k2tog [8 sts].
Cast off. This cast-off row is the base of the
petal.

Outer petals
Knit nine petals.
Cast on 4st in red wool using 3.25mm needles.
Row 1: knit.
Row 2–5: knit, increasing one stitch at the
beginning of each row [8 sts].
Row 6: knit.
Row 7–8: knit, increasing one stitch at the
beginning of each row [10 sts].
Row 9: knit.
Row 10–11: knit, increasing one stitch at the
beginning of each row [12 sts].
Row 12: knit.
Row 13–14: knit, increasing one stitch at the
beginning of each row [14 sts].

Row 15–23: knit.
Row 24–25: knit, decreasing one stitch at the
beginning of each row [12 sts].
Row 26: knit.
Row 27–29: knit, decreasing one stitch at the
beginning of each row [9 sts].
Cast off. This cast-off row is the outer edge of
the petal.

Making up
Cut a length of thin wire twice as long as the
intended length of your rose stem. Weave the
wire across the bottom of the central petal
and then pull the wire ends together and
twist. Repeat for the first petal and then the
second, wrapping each around the central
petal before twisting the wire ends together.
Continue adding petals in this way until you
get to the outer layer. These petals are best
wired on the wrong side of the knitting so that
they can be bent into position. Cut a length
of wire in the same way as before and then
carefully weave it through the knitting on
the reverse side of a petal, close to the outer
edge and following the shape of the petal.
If you are using jewellery wire in the same
colour as the wool then it will be easy to hide
but if you are using silver wire you will have
to work carefully to keep it hidden. Pull the
wire ends down as before and twist them
together. Add the petals to the rose, with the
wire on the underside, and bending the petals
edges over into a pleasing shape. Repeat for
the remaining petals. Twist all the wire ends
together and then bind the wire stem carefully
with another length of wire. Using florist's
tape, and starting close to the petals, wrap the
tape around the stem pulling gently as you
work. Stretching the tape will hold it firmly
around the stem. To make the centre of the
flower, cut a 40cm (16in) length of wool and
wrap it round and round one finger. Gently
remove it from your finger, taking care that it
keeps its shape. Add fabric glue to the centre
of the rose and then place the wrapped wool

carefully onto the glue. Make a gap in the wool at the centre of the rose and then add another blob of glue. Carefully place a pearl on to the glue, holding it in position until the glue gets tacky. To add sparkle to the petal, dab the edges with fabric glue and then sprinkle with red glitter. When the glue is completely dry, shake off any loose glitter.

PHONE COVER

Finished off with a vintage button, this knitted case is sure to be admired. It will also help keep your mobile phone safe

Materials:
Merino wool – green, pink and cream
Button

Needles:
1 pair 4mm (UK 8; US 6) knitting needles

Instructions:

Cast on 34 sts in green wool using 4mm needles.
Row 1–4: st st, starting with a knit row.
Row 5–6: change to pink and continue in st st.
Row 7: change to green, knit.
Row 8: change to cream, purl.
Row 9–10: change back to green, knit 2 rows in st st.
Row 11: k3 in green (k1 pink, k4 green) twice, k1 pink, k6 green, (k1 pink, k4 green) twice, k1 pink, k3 green.
Row 12: p2 green, (p3 pink, p2 green) 3 times, p2 green, (p3 pink, p2 green) 3 times.
Row 13: (k2 green, k3 pink) 3 times, k4 green, (k3 pink, k2 green) 3 times.
Row 14: (p2 green, p1 pink, p1 green, p1 pink) 3 times, p4 green, (p1 pink, p1 green, p1 pink, p2 green) 3 times.
Row 15–16: change to green and continue in st st.
Row 17: *k1 green, (k1 cream, k4 green) 3 times, k1 green, (k1 cream, k4 green) 3 times, k1 cream, k1 green.
Row 18–22: change to green and continue in st st.*
Row 23–28: repeat rows 17–22 from * to *.
Row 29–34: repeat rows 17–22 from * to *.
Row 35: change to pink and knit.
Row 36: cast off 17 sts in purl, purl to the end of the row [17 sts].
Row 37: change to green and knit row.
Row 38: purl.
Row 39: (k1 green, k1 cream) across the row.
Row 40: change to green and purl.
Row 41–42: change to green and work 2 rows in st st.
Row 43–44: repeat rows 39 and 40.
Row 45: k2 green, (k1 pink, k1 green, k1 pink) to last 2 sts, k2 tog.
Row 46: (p2 green, p3 pink), 3 times, to last 2 sts, purl in green.
Row 47: (k2 green, k3 pink), 3 times to last 2 sts, knit in green.
Row 48: p3 green, p1 pink, p4 green, p1 pink, p4 green, p1 pink, p3 green.
Row 49: change to green and continue in st st.
Row 50: p8 sts, cast off 3 sts, purl to the end of the row.
Row 51: k7 sts, cast on 3 sts, knit to the end of the row.
Row 52: purl.
Row 53: change to pink and knit row.
Row 54: cast off in pink on a purl row.

Making up

On the wrong side of the knitting, fold the front over onto the back of the phone cover. Carefully sew along the bottom edge and up the side seam. Turn the cover through to the right side. Stitch a button to the front of the cover to correspond with the buttonhole on the flap.

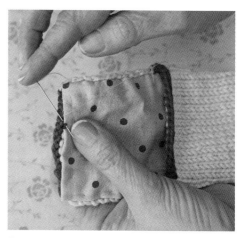

For extra protection why not line the cover with a pretty cotton fabric?

PRETTY FLOWERS

These simple decorative flowers can be attached to clothing as well as your special parcels, boxes and gift tags

Materials: Oddments of wool

Needles: To suit the wool size

Instructions:

Flower
Cast on 41 sts using the thumb method of casting on.
Row 1: k1 *cast off 6 sts (2 sts left on needle)* repeat from * to * 5 times to last stitch, k1.
Cut the wool and thread it through the remaining 11 sts.
Pull up tightly and fasten off securely.

Use the flowers to decorate tags, bags and boxes. Finish with a button or bead.

DOLL'S HAT AND SCARF

Using fine wool will create the right scale for this fashion doll

Materials:
Fine mohair – red, cream
Pearl beads

Needles:
1 pair 3.25mm (UK 10; US 3) knitting needles

Instructions:

Scarf
Cast on 8 sts using cream mohair and 3.25mm needles.
Work in st st for 2.5cm (1in).
Change to red mohair and knit in st st for 23cm (9in).
Change to cream mohair and work in st st for 2.5cm (1in).
Cast off.

Hat
Cast on 20 sts using cream mohair and 3.25mm needles. Work in st st for 8 rows. Change to red mohair and work 6 rows in st st. Break yarn, leaving a long end. Thread through the stitches on the needle and pull up tightly and secure.

Making up
To make the fringed edge, fold a length of cream wool in half, and thread a large-eyed sewing needle with the folded end. On the edge of the scarf, working from the wrong side, bring the folded wool end to the right side of the scarf and slip the needle off the wool. Put the cut ends of the wool through the loop and pull tightly. Make five more loops across the scarf edge. Repeat for the other end of the scarf. Trim the fringe to the same length - see page 35. To embroider the scarf, thread a large-eyed needle with red wool, and make long stitches in a star shape on one end of the scarf - see the knitting notes on page 7. Sew a pearl bead in the centre. Repeat for the other end of the scarf. To make a bobble for the hat, cut a length of wool to hold the bobble together (the fastener), and lay it along a pencil. Wind another longer length of wool around and around the pencil for about 3cm (1¼in). Pull the fastener ends together, and tie in a loose knot around the loops of wool. Slip the loops off the pencil. Cut through the loops and then knot the fastener tightly. Trim the bobble neatly and sew it onto the hat - see the knitting notes on page 6.

31

RAG DOLL

Old buttons and flecked wool give this doll a wonderful vintage look. Knit the hat and scarf to keep her warm

Materials:
Aran knitting wool – cream, green
Crochet thread – gold
Scraps of brown wool for the hair
Toy stuffing
Buttons
Small amount of stranded cotton or wool to embroider the doll's face – brown, pink

Needles:
1 pair 5mm (UK 6; US8) knitting needles
1 pair 3.25mm (UK 10; US3) knitting needles

Instructions:

Dress
Make two dresses.
Starting at the bottom edge of the dress cast on 10 sts in green wool using 5mm needles and work in st st.
Row 1–4: knit in st st.
Row 5–6: change to cream wool and continue in st st.
Row 7–8: change to green wool and continue in st st.
Row 9–10: change to cream wool and continue in st st.
Row 11: change to green wool, k2tog, k6, k2tog [8 sts].
Row 12: purl.
Row 13: k2tog, k4, k2tog [6 sts].
Row 14: purl.
Row 15: k2tog, k2, k2tog [4 sts].
Row 16: purl.
Cast off.

Arms and legs
Make two arms and two legs, reversing the wool colours for each.
Starting at the top edge of the arm or leg cast on 6 sts in green or cream wool using 5mm needles.
Row 1–10: work in st st.
Row 11–14: change colour and work in st st.

Break yarn, leaving a long end. Thread through the stitches on the needle, then pull up tightly and secure.

Head
Cast on 6 sts in cream wool using 5mm needles.
Row 1: knit into the front and back of every stitch [12 sts].
Row 2–8: st st.
Row 9: k2tog across the row [6 sts].
Break yarn, leaving a long end. Thread through the stitches on the needle, then pull up tightly and secure.

Scarf
Cast on 3 sts in green wool using 5mm needles.
Row 1–45: knit.
Cast off.

Hat
Cast on 26 sts in gold crochet thread using 3.25mm needles.
Row 1–4: knit.
Row 5–9: st st.
Row 10: (k2tog, k2) to the last 2 sts, k2tog [19 sts].
Row 11: purl.
Row 12: (k2tog, k2) to last st, k1 [14 sts].
Row 13: purl.
Break yarn, leaving a long end. Thread through the stitches on the needle, then pull up tightly and secure.

Making up
Working on the wrong side of the knitted head, sew the back edges together leaving a small gap. Turn to the right side, stuff, and then sew up the gap to make a ball shape. Starting at the gathered end of the arms and legs, and working on the wrong side of the knitting, sew up the back seams. Turn the arm or leg through to the right side. Stitch across the top edge. Working on the wrong

side of the dress, sew the side seams and the neck edge together. Turn through to the right side, stuff and then place the legs just inside the opening at the bottom of the dress. Sew along the edge, securing the legs in the seam. Sew the arms and the head to the dress. The hair is made by cutting individual lengths of wool. They are threaded into a needle and then taken through the knitting at the centre parting and knotted once. Add the individual wool lengths working from the front of the doll's head to the back. The wool ends are then pulled down at either side of the doll's head and plaited. The doll's eyes and mouth are French knots worked in wool or stranded cotton - see the knitting notes on page 7. The back seam of the hat is sewn up on the wrong side of the knitting. Finish by sewing a button on to both ends of the scarf and then wrap it around the doll's neck like a real scarf.

SCOTTIE DOG

Knitted in black wool with a silver fleck, this adorable little Scottie is sure to become a favourite friend

Materials:
Double knitting wool – black
Toy stuffing
Toy eyes and nose with a safety back
Felt – pink
Ribbon

Needles:
1 pair 4mm (UK 8; US 6) knitting needles

Instructions:

Body
Cast on 2 sts using black wool and 4mm needles.
Row 1: knit
Row 2: inc 1 st at the beginning of the row, knit to the end [3 sts].
Row 3: knit.
Row 4: inc 1 st at the beginning of the row, knit to the end [4 sts].
Row 5–7: knit 3 rows.
Row 8: inc 13 sts at the beginning of the row, knit to the end [17 sts].
Row 9: knit.
Row 10: inc 2 sts at the beginning of the row, knit to the end [19 sts].
Row 11: knit.
Row 12: inc 2 sts at the beginning of the row, knit to the end [21 sts].
Row 13: knit.
Row 14: inc 2 sts at the beginning of the row, knit to the end [23 sts].
Row 15–65: knit 51 rows.
Row 66: dec 2 sts at the beginning of the row, knit to the end [21 sts].
Row 67: knit.
Row 68: dec 2 sts at the beginning of the row, knit to the end [19 sts].
Row 69: knit.
Row 70: dec 2 sts at the beginning of the row, knit to the end [17 sts].
Row 71: knit.
Row 72: dec 13 sts at the beginning of the row, knit to the end [4 sts].
Row 73–75: knit 3 rows.
Row 76: dec 1st at the beginning of the row, knit to the end [3 sts].
Row 77: knit.
Row 78: dec 1st at the beginning of the row, knit to the end [2 sts].
Row 79: knit last 2 sts together. Fasten off.

Head
Cast on 16 sts.
Rows 1–29: knit. Cast off.

Ears (knit 2)
Cast on 2 sts.
Row 1: knit.
Row 2: inc 1 st at the beginning of the row, knit to the end [3 sts].
Row 3: knit.
Row 4: inc 1 st at the beginning of the row, knit to the end [4 sts].
Row 5–9: knit 5 rows.
Row 10: dec 1 st at the beginning of the row, knit to the end [3 sts].
Row 11: knit.
Row 12: dec 1 st at the beginning of the row, knit to the end [2 sts].
Row 13: knit.
Cut the wool and pull through the stitches.

Back panel
*Cast on 9 sts
Row 1–2: knit 2 rows.
Row 3: k2tog, knit to last 2 sts, k2tog [7sts].
Row 4: knit.
Row 5: k2tog, knit to last 2 sts, k2tog [5sts].
Row 6–13: knit 8 rows.
Row 14: k2tog, k1, k2tog [3sts].*
Row 15–24: knit 10 rows.
Row 25: k3tog. Fasten off.

Front Panel
Work as front panel from * to *.
Row 15–41: knit 27 rows.
Row 42: k3tog. Fasten off.

Continued on page 36

To make the Scottie's fringe, thread a needle with the folded end of a length of wool. On the RS of the knitting make a small stitch. Slip the needle off the wool. Put the cut wool ends through the loop and pull up tightly. Continue adding fringe. Trim to the desired length.

SCOTTIE DOG

Making up

Fold the body so that the top edges meet. Sew the Scottie together along the centre back, and then up and over the tail, but not the sloping neck edge or the front and back seams. Fold the head in half so that the knitted rows are horizontal. Sew up the back seam and then across the top of the head, stopping at the nose. About half of the bottom seam of the Scottie's head should be stitched to the sloping neck edge on the body and the other half will form the Scottie's chin, which juts out. Sew the front panel in place, working from the nose to the chin, then chin to the neck and then down the front. When you get to the bottom you will find that there is enough body to be stitched across the bottom of the front panel. Stitch up the other side of the panel, attaching it to the body and head as before. Stitch the triangular back panel under the Scottie's tail, down one side and along the bottom but leaving one seam open. Turn the Scottie through the gap to the right side and stuff lightly. If you are adding toy eyes and a nose with safely backs then you will need to do so at this point. Sew up the remaining seam. Cut a small tongue from pink felt and stitch it halfway down the front seam below the Scottie's nose. To make the fringe, cut a length of black wool, fold it in half and then thread the folded end through a large-eyed needle. On the right side of the knitting make a small stitch. The looped end must come all the way through to the right side of the knitting. Slip the needle off the wool. Put the cut ends through the loop and pull up firmly. Continue adding fringe in this way. Repeat along the nose, under the chin, above the eyebrows and at the front and back for the skirt. Cut the wool ends level and then tease them out. As a finishing touch tie a length of ribbon around the Scottie's neck.

KNITTED PURSE

This pretty little purse is a great gift for a child to keep their pocket money or tiny treasured toys

Materials:
Merino knitting wool – mauve, mustard
Wooden button
Wooden beads

Needles:
1 pair 3.25mm (UK 10; US 3) knitting needles

Instructions:

Cast on 24 sts in mauve wool using 3.25mm needles.
Knit in g st until your work measures 20cm(8in).
Change to mustard coloured wool and dec 1 st at either end of this, and every other row, until 12 sts remain.
Knit 1 row.
Buttonhole rows from * to *.
Next row: *k2tog, k3, cast off 2 sts, k3, k2tog [8 sts].
Next row: k4, cast on 2 sts, k4 [10 sts]*.

Next row: knit, dec 1 st at either end [8 sts].
Continue in g st, dec 1 st at either end of every other row until 2 sts remain.
k2tog. Fasten off.

i-cord handle
Make an i-cord using the instructions on page 6. It should be long enough to make a handle for the purse when folded in half.

Making up
Fold the knitting so that the flap is at the top of the purse. Sew the side seams together and then turn through to the right side. Fold the i-cord in half and then stitch it just inside the purse on the side seam. Sew a button on the purse front to correspond with the buttonhole on the flap. Using mustard coloured wool, embroider lazy daisy stitches in groups of four on the front of the purse - see the knitting notes on page 7. Stitch a bead in the centre of each flower.

PEACH & CHOCOLATE CUPCAKE

Put this yummy cupcake on a cake stand, displayed on a vintage dresser, and it will look almost good enough to eat

Materials:
Double knitting wool – cream, peach, chocolate
100% cotton 4 ply – white
60mm (2¼in) polystyrene craft ball
Seed beads for decoration – shades of brown
Toy stuffing

Needles:
1 pair 4mm (UK 8; US 6) knitting needles
1 pair 2.25mm (UK 13; US 1) knitting needles

Instructions:

Side of case
Cast on 60 sts using 4 ply white cotton and 2.25mm needles.
Row 1–11: k1, p1 across the row for 11 rows.
Row 12: inc every second purl stitch across the row.
Cast off.

Base of case
Cast on 10 sts using 4 ply white cotton and 2.25mm needles. Work in st st.
Row 1: * purl.
Row 2: knit, increasing 1 st at beg and end of row [12 sts]. *
Rows 3–8: repeat from * to * 3 times [18 sts].
Rows 9–11: continue in st st.
Rows 12–18: dec 1 st at beg and end of every k row [10 sts].
Row 19: purl.
Cast off.

Top of cake
Cast on 40 sts in cream double knitting wool using 4mm needles.
Row 1–10: st st for 10 rows.
Row 11: knit, decreasing 6 sts randomly across the row [34 sts].
Row 12: knit
Row 13: knit, decreasing 6 sts randomly across the row [28 sts].

Row 14: knit
Row 15: knit, decreasing 4 sts randomly across the row [24 sts].
Row 16: knit.
Break yarn, leaving a long end. Thread through the stitches on the needle and pull up tightly.

Iced topping
Cast on 2 sts in peach double knitting wool using 4mm needles.
Row 1: *cast on 2 sts at the beg of row [4 sts], then cast off those 2 sts, k1 [2 sts].
Row 2: knit.*
Repeat these two rows from * to * 106 times in peach.
Change to cream wool and repeat these two rows a further 12 times.
Cast off.

Chocolate ball
Cast on 6 sts in brown double knitting wool using 4mm needles.
Row 1: k1, increase into the next 4 sts across the row, k1 [10 sts].
Row 2: k1, increase into the next 8 sts across the row, k1 [18 sts].
Row 3–7: knit.
Row 8: k1, k2tog to the last stitch, k1 [10 sts].
Row 9: k1, k2tog to last stitch, k1 [6 sts].
Cast off.

Making up
Join the side seam of the cupcake case and then carefully stitch the bottom in place from the outside. Join the side seam of the cupcake top. Pull up the thread at the top of the cake and take it through to the wrong side of the knitting before darning in place. Insert the polystyrene ball into the cupcake top, pushing a small amount of toy stuffing around the inside edges of the cupcake case. Put the top and bottom together and then adjust the stuffing so that it fits neatly. Sew the top and bottom of the cupcake together with small invisible stitches. Pin the strip of iced topping

onto the top of the cupcake, starting on the lower edge. Wind the strip around the cake top, pinning as you work. Using peach wool, catch-stitch the bobble strip firmly to the cake top, finishing with the cream bobbles at the top. Stuff the chocolate ball and, using the starting and finishing wool ends, close the side seam and the top and bottom. Stitch the ball to the top of the cupcake, adding a few seed beads for decoration.

MUG COSY

This pretty mug cosy will keep your drink snug whilst you finish your knitting. It's easy to adapt to any size

Materials:
Double knitting wool – blue, pink
Pearl buttons – two

Needles:
1 pair 4mm (UK 8; US 6) knitting needles

Instructions:

Cast on 62 sts in blue double knitting wool, the background colour, using 4mm needles.
Row 1–3: work in rib (knit 1, purl 1).
Row 4–17: follow the charted pattern for 14 rows working in stocking stitch and using both wool colours. The chart shows the complete design.
Row 18: work in st st in the background colour.
Row 19–20: work in rib (knit 1, purl 1) in the background colour, starting with a knit stitch.
Cast off in rib.

This pattern fits a mug with a 27cm (10⅝in) circumference and the cosy should fit snugly around your mug. To make a smaller or larger cosy just reduce or increase the number of background stitches, evenly, at the beginning and end of the pattern.

To make up the mug cosy
Make two buttonhole loops on the edge of the cosy, at the top and bottom - see the instructions below. Sew two buttons on the opposite edge to correspond with the loops.

Buttonhole loop
Thread a blunt ended needle with wool in the background colour. Tie a knot in the end of the wool and, starting on the edge of the knitting at the top of the mug cosy, make two straight stitches the same size as the button to form a loop. Make sure you start and finish the loop at the same point. Work buttonhole stitch over the loop, bringing the wool to the left of the needle. Insert the needle under the loop and over the yarn. Pull up and continue until the bar is tightly covered. To finish, take the wool end to the inside of the cosy, weave it through the knitting and cut off neatly.

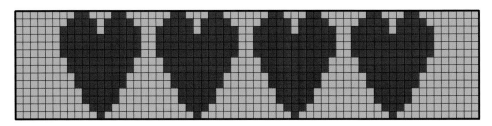

BIRD PINS

Cute and easy to knit in cotton yarn, these popular British birds look great pinned to clothing and accessories

Materials:
Cotton knitting yarn – peach, beige, pink
Felt for backing and beak – pink, brown
Buttons and beads for eyes
Brooch back

Needles:
I pair of 3.25mm (UK 10; US 3) knitting needles

Instructions:

To knit the owl
Cast on 6 sts using peach knitting yarn and 3.25mm knitting needles and work in st st.
Row 1: kfb across the row (knit into the front and back of each stitch) [12 sts].
Row 2–8: st st starting with a purl row.
Row 9: k2tog across the row [6 sts].
Row 10: purl
Row 11: knit into the front and back of each stitch across row [12 sts].
Row 12: purl.
Row 13: kfb into first and last stitch [14 sts].
Row 14: purl.
Cast off.

To knit the robin
Cast on 6 sts in beige knitting yarn and work in st st.
Row 1: kfb across row [12 sts].
Row 2: purl
Row 3: k4 beige, k4 pink, k4 beige.
Row 4: p3 beige, p6 pink, p3 beige.
Row 5: k2 beige, k8pink, k2 beige.
Row 6: p2 beige, p8 pink, p2 beige.
Row 7: k2 beige, k8 pink, k2 beige.
Row 8: p3 beige, p6 pink, p3 beige.
Row 9: k4 beige, k4 pink, k4 beige.
Row 10: working in beige, purl to the end of the row.
Row 11: k2tog, k8, k2tog [10 sts].
Row 12: p2tog, p6, p2tog [8 sts].
Row 13: k2tog 4 times [4 sts].
Cast off.

To knit the wings
Cast on 1 st in beige or peach knitting yarn.
Row 1: knit
Row 2: purl
Row 3: kfb [2 sts].
Row 4: purl.
Row 5: kfb of both stitches [4 sts].
Row 6–11: st st starting with a purl row.
Cut yarn and weave it through remaining 4 sts.

To make the legs and tail
Cut three long lengths of yarn and tie a knot at one end to hold them together. Plait until long enough to dangle down below the bird when folded in half. Secure with a knot. Cut off the yarn ends neatly.

Making up
Secure all the yarn ends by weaving them through the back of the knitting. Fold the legs in half and stitch them to the back of the knitted bird so that they dangle down. Stitch the wings to either side of the bird.
Cut a small triangle of felt for the bird's beak. This should be attached using small neat stitches in matching sewing thread. Stitch buttons or beads either side of the nose for the eyes. Lightly stretch the knitted bird and pin it to felt. Cut around the bird as close as you can to the knitting. Use fabric glue or small neat stitches to attach the felt to the back of the brooch. Attach the brooch back.

You could attach these pretty birds to the front of a greetings card. The robin would make a very attractive Christmas card pinned to a blue handmade paper background, decorated with gold stars. Try twisting sparkly embroidery thread with the yarn to give a seasonal feel.

COUNTRY HEART

This country heart door hanger, decorated with vintage buttons, will look lovely displayed on an old pine door

Materials:
Double knitting wool – cream, pink, blue
Pearl beads
Buttons
Toy stuffing

Needles:
1 pair 4mm (UK 8; US 6) knitting needles

Instructions:

Heart
Make two heart shapes.
Cast on 2 sts using cream double knitting wool and 4mm needles.
Row 1: knit.
Row 2: increase 1 st at both ends of the row [4 sts].
Row 3: increase 1 st at both ends of the row [6 sts].
Row 4: increase 1 st at both ends of the row [8 sts].
Row 5: increase 1 st at both ends of the row [10 sts].
Row 6: increase 1 st at both ends of the row [12 sts].
Row 7: increase 1 st at both ends of the row [14 sts].
Row 8: increase 1 st at both ends of the row [16 sts].
Row 9: increase 1 st at both ends of the row [18 sts].
Row 10: increase 1 st at both ends of the row [20 sts].
Row 11–14: knit.
Row 15: increase 1 st at both ends of the row [22 sts].
Row 16: increase 1 st at both ends of the row [24 sts].
Row 17–22: knit.
Row 23: increase 1 st at both ends of the row [26 sts].
Row 24–41: knit 18 rows.
Row 42: decrease 1 st at both ends of the row [24 sts].
Row 43: decrease 1 st at both ends of the row [22 sts].
Row 44: k2tog, k7, cast off 4, k7, k2tog.
Put one group of 8 stitches onto a safety pin or clip and work on the other 8 stitches.
Row 1: *k to last 2 sts, k2tog [7 sts].
Row 2: k5, k2tog [6 sts].
Row 3: knit.
Row 4: knit to last 2 sts, k2tog [5 sts].
Row 5: knit.
Row 6: k2tog, k1, k2tog [3 sts]. Cast off.*
Remove the remaining 8 stitches from the safety pin or clip and, working from the outer edge, repeat from * to *.

Bow
Cast on 7 sts using pink wool.
Knit 25 rows, cast off.

Bow Centre
Cast on 3 sts using cream wool.
Knit 10 rows, cast off.

Patch
Cast on 7 sts using cream wool.
Knit 12 rows, cast off.

Flower
Make a flower in blue wool using the instructions on page 30.

Tassel
Make the tassel following the instructions on the facing page.

Making up
Place the front and back of the heart together and, using cream wool, sew around the edges, leaving a gap for turning. Turn to the right side and then stuff before sewing up the gap. Make a plait using cream wool and then attach this to the top of the heart. Using the wool end attached to the tassel, sew it to the bottom of the heart. Wrap the bow centre

Making a tassel

Wrap cream wool around four fingers on one hand about 20 times. Cut through the wool bundle and lay it flat on the table. Place a length of wool under the bundle at the mid-point, and tie it in a knot. Leave the wool ends uncut as they will be used to attach the tassel to the heart. Then bring the bundle ends together to form a tassel. Wrap a length of wool around the tassel about 1.5cm (⅝in) down from the folded top. Tie in a nice firm knot, trim the ends and smooth them down into the bundle.

around the bow and secure it to the bow back with a few stitches. Sew the bow to the front of the heart. Stitch the patch in place using large stitches in pink wool. Sew the flower to the front of the heart with a pearl bead in the centre. Stitch buttons in the gaps.

This heart would make a lovely decoration for the Christmas tree. Use shades of red and green wool, adding bells and gold beads. For extra sparkle use gold or silver crochet or embroidery thread. It's a great hostess gift wrapped in tissue paper and tied with ribbon.

TOOTH FAIRY BAG

On the day when your little girl loses her first tooth, give her this pretty knitted bag to help keep her money safe

Materials:
Baby double knitting wool – cream, peach, pink
Net for wings – pink
Felt – flesh coloured and acrylic paints, or wool scraps to embroider the face
Net, fabric or ribbon for the tie

Needles:
1 pair 3.25mm (UK 10; US 3) knitting needles

Instructions:

Bag front
Use the instructions below, or the chart opposite, joining the instructions at row 31.
Cast on 23 sts using cream wool and 3.25mm needles.
Row 1–12: work in st st.
Row 13: *k6 cream, k11 peach, k6 cream.
Row 14: p6 cream, p11 peach, p6 cream.*
Row 15–16: repeat from * to *.
Row 17: **k9 cream, k5 peach, k9 cream.
Row 18: p9 cream, p5 peach, p9 cream.**
Row 19–20: repeat from ** to **.
Row 21: ***k10 cream, k3 pink, k10 cream.
Row 22: p10 cream, p3 pink, p10 cream.***
Row 23–24: repeat from *** to ***.
Row 25: repeat row 21.
Row 26–30: using cream wool work in st st for 5 rows, starting with a purl row.
Row 31: (k3, yf, k2tog) 4 times, k3.
Row 32–35: continue in st st starting with a purl row.
Cast off on a purl row.

Bag back
Cast on 23 sts using cream wool and 3.25mm needles.
Row 1–30: work in st st using cream wool.
Row 31: (k3, yf, k2tog) 4 times, k3.
Row 32–35: continue in st st starting with a purl row.
Cast off on a purl row.

Making up
Finish off all the wool ends neatly on the wrong side of the knitting. Using peach wool, embroider the fairy's legs and arms using long stitches and the chart opposite. Cut two lengths of pink net approximately 7 x 2.5cm (2¾x1in). Place together and round off the corners at either end to create a wing shape. Thread a darning needle onto one end of the strips and make a stitch behind the fairy's body at the shoulder. Secure on the back of the knitting with a few stitches.

You can either paint a face onto felt or embroider eyes and a mouth using wool or stranded cotton. I cut an oval from flesh coloured felt and used acrylic paints to add face detail. Using fabric glue, stick the felt over the knitted face. To make the hair, cut six lengths of brown stranded cotton or wool and lay them together. Find the middle point and secure firmly together with the same colour wool or thread. Cut the hair to the desired length and sew in place. With wrong sides facing, place the front and back of the bag together. Using cream wool, sew the bag together on three sides, leaving the top open and a small gap on one side seam to act as an extra ribbon hole. Turn the bag through to the right side. Thread ribbon, net or fabric through the holes, pull up and tie with a knot.

Use the chart opposite to knit the fairy design

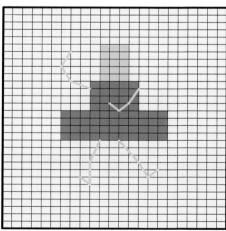

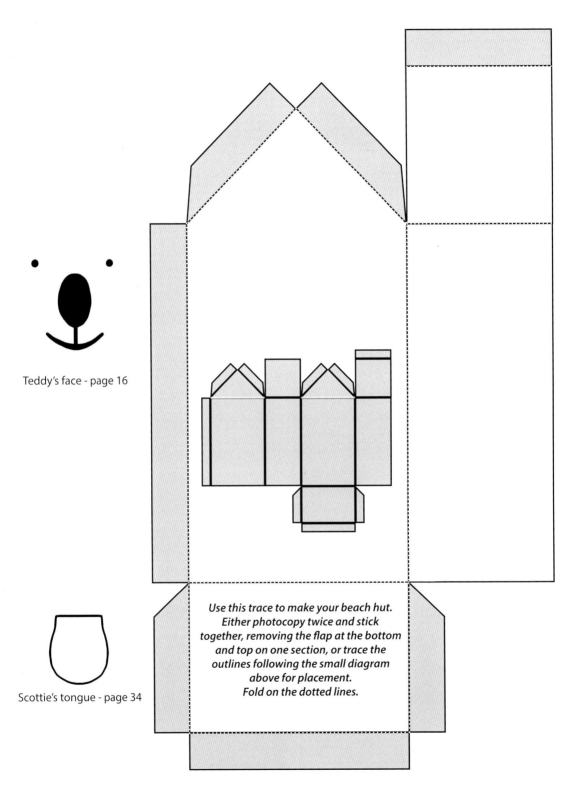

Teddy's face - page 16

Scottie's tongue - page 34

Use this trace to make your beach hut.
Either photocopy twice and stick
together, removing the flap at the bottom
and top on one section, or trace the
outlines following the small diagram
above for placement.
Fold on the dotted lines.

Beach hut paperweight - page 10